great

QUOTES

from

GREAT WOMEN

This collection of quotations is dedicated to all the great women whose words have motivated, inspired and brought tears and laughter into our lives.

This book was compiled by someone who truly believes in the power of words and how they can impact feelings and attitudes. We hope you enjoy the quotations as much as we do.

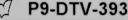

ISBN: 1-880461-04-8

"I gain strength, courage and confidence by every experience in which I must stop and look fear in the face. . . I say to myself, I've lived through this and can take the next thing that comes along. . . We must do the things we think we cannot do."

Eleanor Roosevelt

"I never notice
what has been done.
I only see what
remains to be done."

Madam Curie

"Far away there in the
sunshine are my highest
aspirations. I may not
reach them, but I can look up
and see their beauty, believe
in them and try to follow
where they lead."

Louisa May Alcott

"Every great
mistake has a halfway
moment, a split
second when it can be
recalled and perhaps
remedied."

Pearl S. Buck

"Being powerful is
like being a
lady. If you have to
tell people you are,
you aren't."

Margaret Thatcher

"To love what you
do and feel that it
matters — how
could anything be
more fun?"

Katherine Graham

"The first problem
for all of us,
men and women,
is not to learn but
to unlearn."

Gloria Steinem

"Don't be humble: you're not that great."

Golda Meir

"From birth to age 18,
a girl needs good
parents, from 18 to 35
she needs good looks,
from 35 to 55 she needs
a good personality,
and from 55 on she
needs cash."

Sophie Tucker

"Yesterday is a
cancelled check; tomorrow
is a promissory note;
today is the only cash
you have — so spend
it wisely."

Kay Lyons

"Men, their rights and nothing more; women, their rights and nothing less."

Susan B. Anthony

". . .perhaps one has to be very old before one learns how to be amused rather than shocked."

Pearl S. Buck

"Nothing in
life is to be feared.
It is only to be
understood."

Madame Curie

"Opportunities
are usually disguised
by hard work, so
most people don't
recognize them."

Ann Landers

"It is not fair to ask of others what you are not willing to do yourself."

Eleanor Roosevelt

"Courage is
the price that
life exacts for
granting peace."

Amelia Earhart

"After the verb 'To love', 'To help' is the most beautiful verb in the world."

Bertha Von Suttner

"We've chosen the path to equality, don't let them turn us around."

Geraldine A. Ferraro

"We are not interested in the possibilities of defeat."

Queen Victoria

"I am only one;
but still I am one. I
cannot do everything, but
still I can do something;
I will not refuse to do the
something I can do."

Helen Keller

GREAT WOMEN

"Loneliness is the most terrible poverty."

Mother Teresa

"You have to
accept whatever comes
and the only important
thing is that you meet
it with courage and with
the best you have
to give."

Eleanor Roosevelt

"We fought hard.
We gave it our best.
We did what was
right. And we made
a difference."

Geraldine Ferraro

"Aerodynamically
the bumble bee shouldn't
be able to fly, but the
bumble bee doesn't know it
so it goes on flying
anyway."

Mary Kay Ash

GREAT
WOMEN

"The more I traveled
the more I realized
that fear makes
strangers of people
who should be
friends."

Shirley MacLaine

"God knows (she knows) that women try."

Gloria Steinem

"In passing, also I would like to say that the first time Adam had a chance he laid the blame on women."

Lady Nancy Astor

"Success can make you
go one of two ways. It can
make you a prima donna,
or it can smooth the
edges, take away the
insecurities, let the nice
things come out."

Barbara Walters

"I've never sought
success in order to get
fame and money; it's
the talent and the
passion that count
in success."

Ingrid Bergman

"A happy woman
is one who has
no cares at all; a
cheerful woman is one
who has cares but
doesn't let them get
her down."

Beverly Sills

"We all live with
the objective of being
happy; our lives are all
different and yet
the same."

Anne Frank

"The most exciting
thing about women's
liberation is that this
century will be able to take
advantage of talent and
potential genius that have
been wasted because
of taboos."

Helen Reddy

"It is worse than
folly. . . not to
recognize the truth,
for in it lies the tinder
for tomorrow."

Pearl S. Buck

"When you cease
to make a
contribution you
begin to die."

Eleanor Roosevelt

"Those who do not know how to weep with their whole heart don't know how to laugh either."

Golda Meir

"Self-expression must pass into communication for its fulfillment."

Pearl S. Buck

"God does not ask
your ability or your
inability. He asks only
your availability."

Mary Kay Ash

"Don't compromise yourself. You are all you've got."

Betty Ford

"Character contributes to beauty. It fortifies a woman as her youth fades. A mode of conduct, a standard of courage, discipline, fortitude and integrity can do a great deal to make a woman beautiful."

Jacqueline Bisset

"Men have always
detested women's
gossip because they
suspect the truth:
their measurements are
being taken and
compared."

Erica Jong

"I've had an
exciting life; I
married for love and
got a little money
along with it."

Rose Kennedy

"This became
a credo of
mine. . . attempt
the impossible
in order to improve
your work."

Bette Davis

"Let the world know
you as you are, not
as you think you should
be, because sooner
or later, if you are posing,
you will forget the
pose, and then where
are you?"

Fanny Brice

"The future belongs to those who believe in the beauty of their dreams."

Eleanor Roosevelt

". . .you don't get to choose how you're going to die, or when. You can only decide how you're going to live. Now!"

Joan Baez

"You grow up
the day you have
your first real laugh
– at yourself."

Edith Barrymore

"When people say:
She's got
everything. I've only
one answer: I haven't
had tomorrow."

Elizabeth Taylor

". . .love is the
only thing that we
can carry with
us when we go, and it
makes the end
so easy."

Louisa May Alcott

"Trouble is a
part of life, and if you
don't share it, you
don't give the person who
loves you a chance to love
you enough."

Dinah Shore

"People who
fight fire with fire
usually end up
with ashes."

Abigail VanBuren

"You cannot
shake hands with
a clenched fist."

Indira Gandhi

"Whether women
are better than men I
cannot say —but I can
say they are certainly
no worse."

Golda Meir

"It isn't the common man at all who is important: it's the uncommon man."

Lady Nancy Astor

"In spite of the
cost of living, it's
still popular."

Kathleen Norris

"Success to me is
having ten honeydew
melons and eating
only the top half of
each one."

Barbara Streisand

"I keep the telephone of my mind open to peace, harmony, health, love and abundance. Then whenever doubt, anxiety, or fear try to call me, they keep getting a busy signal and soon they'll forget my number."

Edith Armstrong

"I don't know anything about luck. I've never banked on it, and I'm afraid of people who do. Luck to me is something else; hard work and realizing what is opportunity and what isn't."

Lucille Ball

"Ninety-eight percent
of the adults in this country
are decent, hard-working,
honest Americans. It's
the other lousy two percent
that get all the publicity.
But then we elected them."

Lily Tomlin

"Sometimes when I look at my children I say to myself, 'Lillian, you should have stayed a virgin'."

Lillian Carter

"I never hated a man enough to give him his diamonds back."

Zsa Zsa Gabor

"I've been rich
and I've been poor.
Rich is better."

Sophie Tucker

"Remember, no one can make you feel inferior without your consent."

Eleanor Roosevelt

"To be successful,
a woman has to
be better at her
job than a man."

Golda Meir

"I'm just a person
trapped inside a
woman's body."

Elaine Boosler

"An archeologist is the
best husband a woman
can have; the older
she gets, the more
interested he is in her."

Agatha Christie

"Some people are more turned on by money than they are by love. . .In one respect they're alike. They're both wonderful as long as they last."

Abigail VanBuren

"In society it is etiquette for ladies to have the best chairs and get handed things. In the home the reverse is the case. That is why ladies are more sociable than gentlemen."

Virginia Graham

"You don't seem to
realize that a poor person
who is unhappy is in a better
position than a rich
person who is unhappy.
Because the poor person
has hope. He thinks money
would help."

Jean Kerr

"Laziness
may appear
attractive, but work
gives satisfaction."

Anne Frank

"The important thing
in acting is to be able to
laugh and cry. If I have to
cry, I think of my sex life. If
I have to laugh, I think of
my sex life."

Glenda Jackson

"Old age is like a plane flying through a storm. Once you're aboard, there's nothing you can do."

Golda Meir

"The suburbs were
discovered, quite
by accident, one day in
the early 1940s by a
Welcome Wagon lady
who was lost."

Erma Bombeck

"The trouble
with the rat race
is that even if you win,
you're still a rat."

Lily Tomlin

"It's easy to be independent
when you've got money. But
to be independent when
you haven't got a thing —
that's the Lord's test."

Mahalia Jackson

"I don't want to
live — I want to
love first, and live
incidentally."

Zelda Fitzgerald

"Protocol is not there to dictate to you. It's there to help you. You have to have the courage and security to do it your way."

Barbara Bush

"People see
God every day; they
just don't
recognize him."

Pearl Bailey